FRETBOARD FORMATIONS

Scale and Chord Forms for Advancing Guitarists

by Shaun Mahoney

Introduction

This book is meant to provide visual aids in an effort to help guitar students better understand the guitar fretboard. The diagrams within are visual layouts or "forms" of essential scales and chords for guitarists studying improvisation, and anything related to jazz and/or commercial music. This is not meant to be a music theory book, and although theory concepts are talked about, students will need knowledge of music theory, particularly jazz theory, in order to effectively make use of the content of this book. It should also be stated that this book provides foundational material of which to build upon and does not depict every single scale and chord possibility on the guitar fretboard.

Table of Contents

Chords

Most songs are built on chords and chord progressions. Guitarists playing jazz and/or other styles should know chord forms around the entire neck in order to be fluent performing music. Understanding chord forms on the fretboard is essential for improvisation as well, and improvised linear solos should always be informed by the chord structure of a song. In jazz theory, the basic unit of harmony is the seventh chord which can be divided into three families; major, minor, and dominant. From there, chords branch out becoming more extended.

Triad Forms in Root Position

Learning the triad chord forms
provides a foundation for building
more complex chords and
understanding the guitar neck.

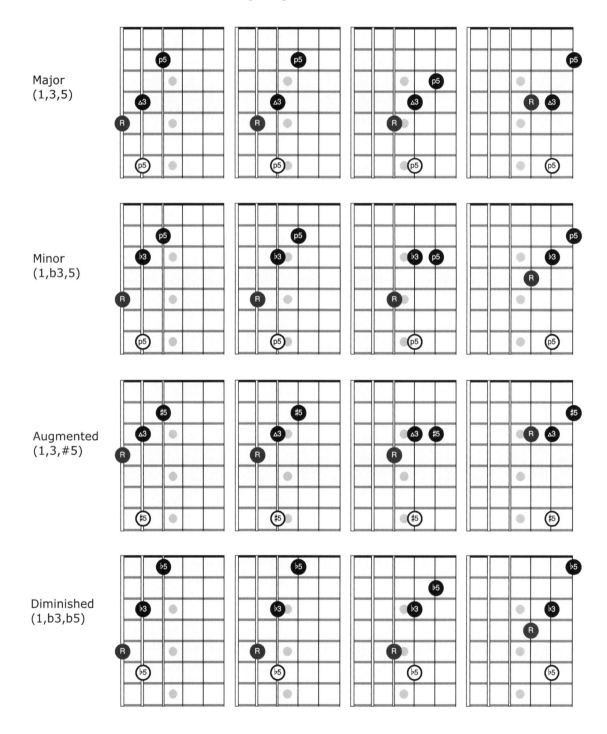

Major
(1,3,5)

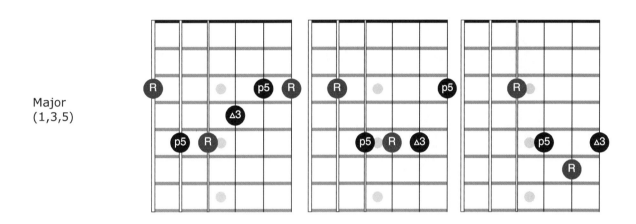

Minor
(1,b3,5)

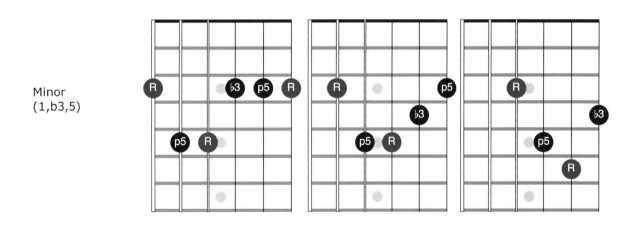

Maj7, Min7, & Dom7 Guide Tone Voicings

Guide tones are the 3rd and 7th of any 7th chord. The guide tones define 7th chords as belonging to the Major, Minor, or Dominant families. Guide tone voicings for the guitar, which include the Root along with the guide tones, are used as a foundation for extended chords.

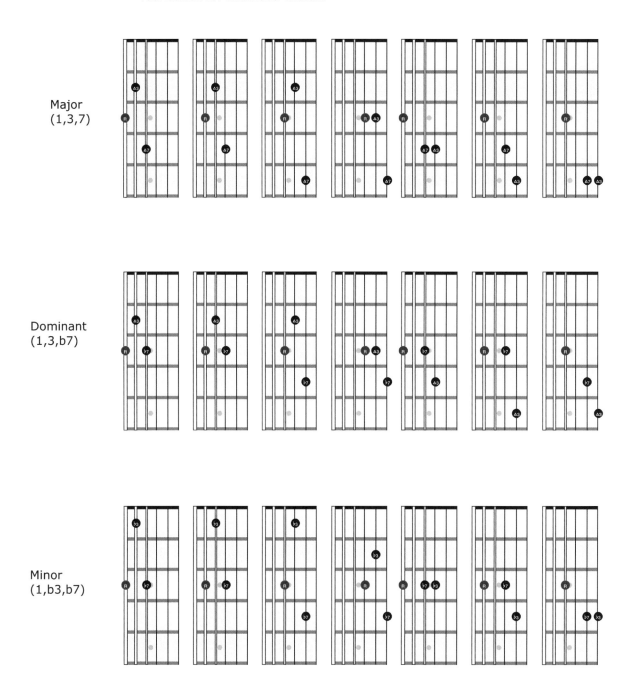

Maj7, Min7, & Dom7 Barre Voicings in Root Position

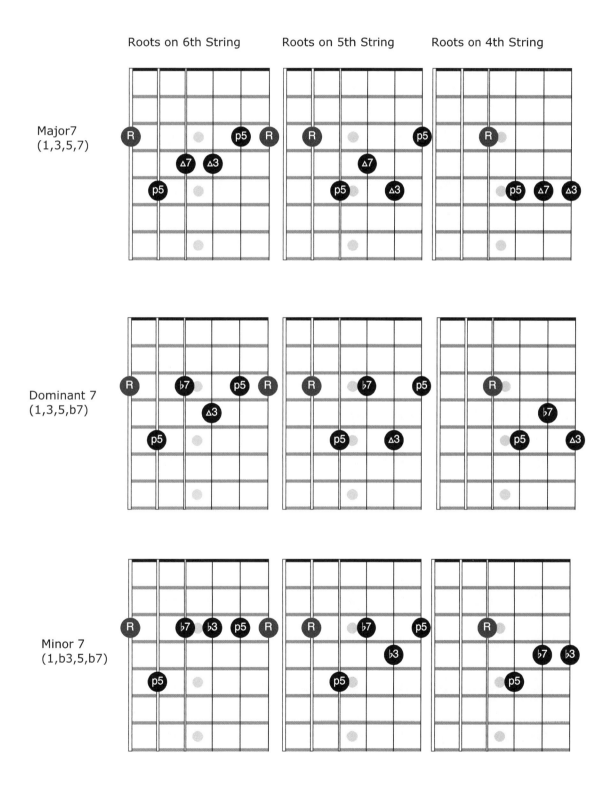

Diminished 7th and Half-Diminished 7th Voicings

Diminished
(1,b3,b5,bb7)

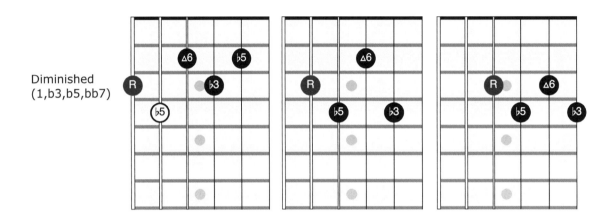

Half-Diminished
(1,b3,b5,b7)

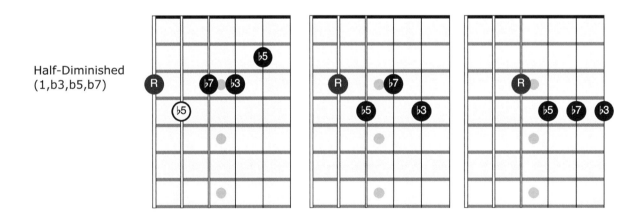

Maj7, Min7, & Dom7 Guide Tone Voicings with Extensions (remember the 2=9th, 4=11th, and 6=13th)

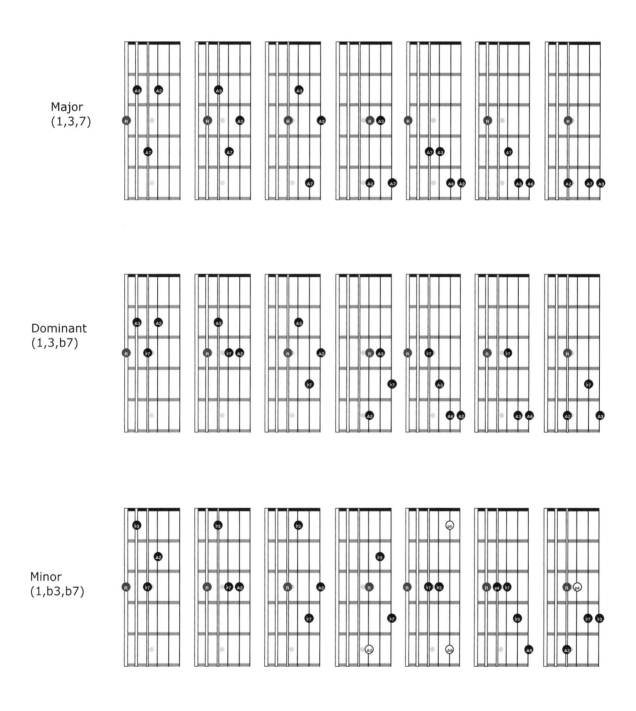

Major Scale and Its Modes

The following major scale forms can be used to map and visualize the major scale and its modes across the entire fretboard. Students should understand how to spell all twelve major scales and understand the major scale modes before applying the forms in this book because the forms will only be useful after understanding the theory behind the scales. The scale forms are used for playing lines of notes, but they are also very important for seeing chordal possibilities, and are necessary to expand chord knowledge. It is imperative to have command of the full visualizaton of the major modes for improvisation because these scales are some of the most basic tools used in music. Since all major scales share the same intervals, the forms of the major scales are the same for all twelve keys. Changing keys can be done by moving the forms up and down the guitar neck to different frets. For the purposes of this book, the scale forms are often presented in the key of G because the key of G easily shows how the forms connect as you move from the bottom to the top of the neck.

Major Scale (diatonic) Forms

The notes from any scale can be mapped out on the guitar neck in almost unlimited combinations. To eliminate much confusion and create a solid foundation for further fretboard study and application, the scales in this book are mapped out in five separate formations. Each form is meant to stay within a 4-6 fret position so that all notes from the scale can be visualized in that particular position. This is true for not only the major scale, but all the scales throughout this book.

In the following pages, these forms will be applied to a few different concepts. The visual memorization of these forms is neccessary for the comprehention and application of major mode studies. The modes of the major scale should be understood in all twelve keys before implementing these forms. I have numbered these forms 1-5 to help connect the forms to diagrams on the following pages.

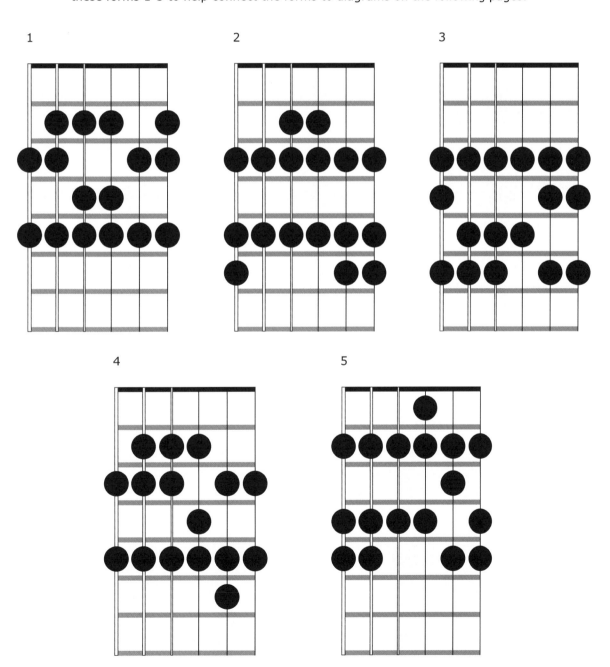

Major Scale Forms Side by Side

By visualizing these forms side by side, it becomes clear how the five forms interlock to connect the major scale throughout the entire neck. The forms repeat after the twelfth fret. It also should be stated that once the major scale modes are understood in theory, these forms will apply to those modes as well. The numbers above each diagram correspond with previous page.

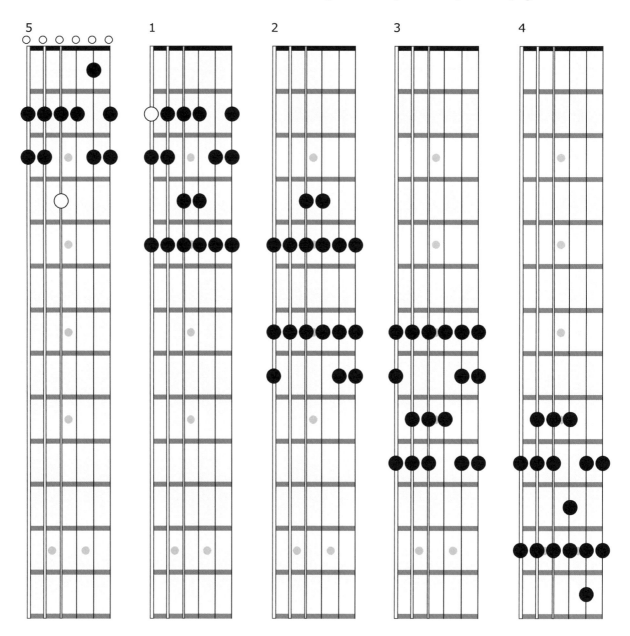

G Major Scale Forms

Five G major forms with scale degree indications:

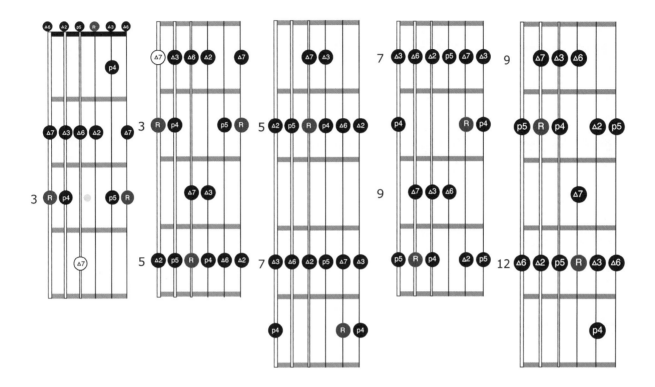

Five G major forms with note names indicated:

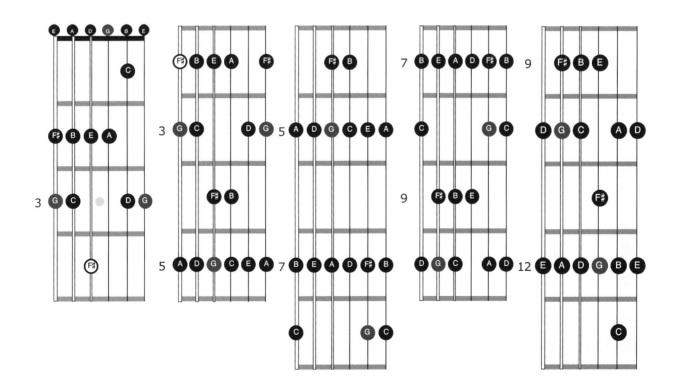

Major Forms Applied to G Ionian

It is important to recognize how
the intervals of the major scale are
layed out on the fretboard.

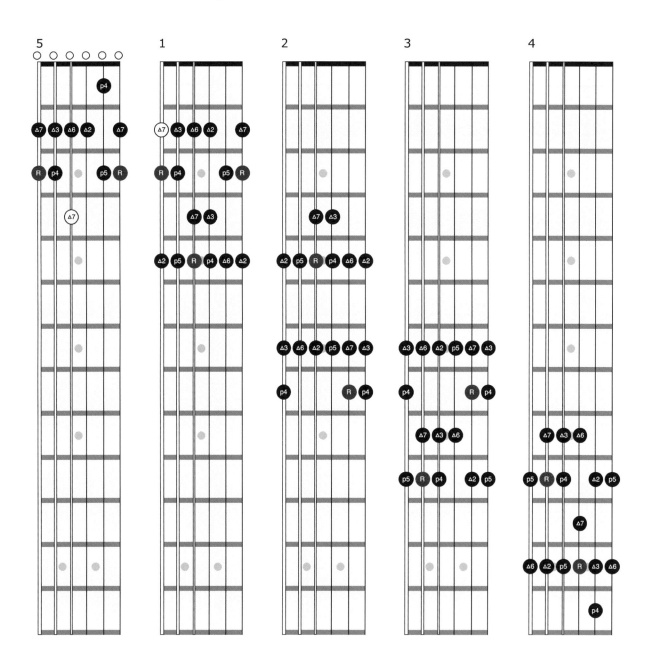

Major forms applied to G Dorian

When applying the major scale forms to different modes, the intervals change to correspond to that particular mode. In this case we have the Dorian mode.

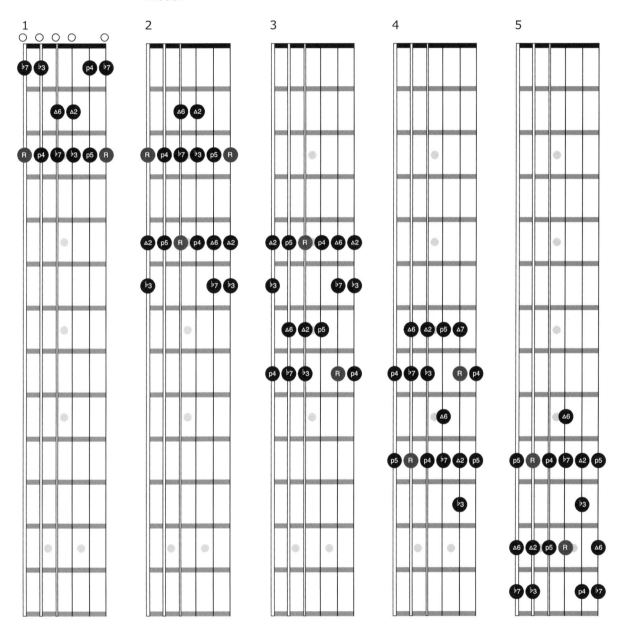

Major forms applied to G mixolydian

The five scale forms are positioned here to map the G mixolydian scale. The intervals of the mixolydian are labeled.

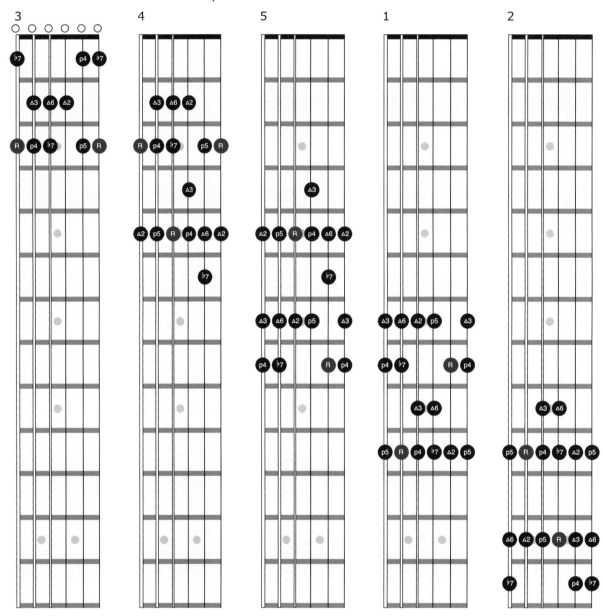

Parrallel Major Modes in G
(with G on string 6)

Notice how all these modes correspond with the 5 major scale forms. All keys and strings can be applied to this concept.

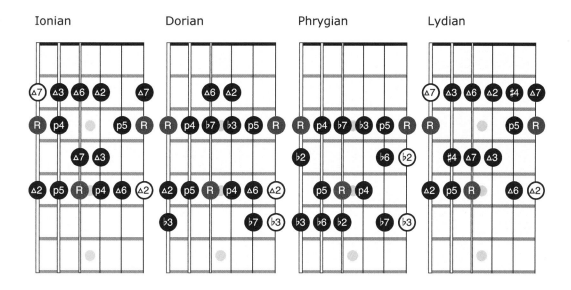

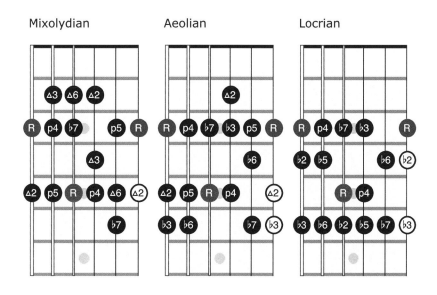

Major 7 Guide Tone Voicings and Corresponding Scale Forms

Fret numbers are applied to G major but the chord and scale forms will correspond on any fret for all keys.

Guide Tone Voicings   Corresponding Scale Forms

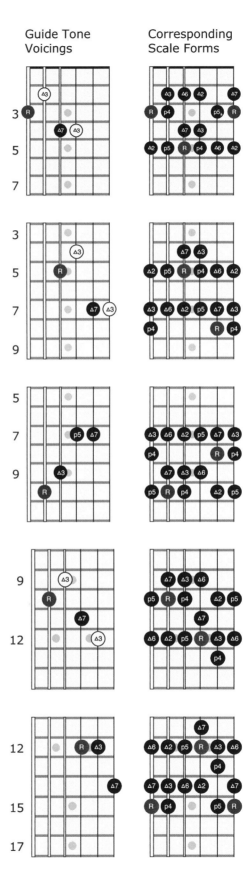

Minor 7 Guide Tone Voicings and Corresponding Dorian Scale Forms

Fret numbers are applied to G minor7 but the chord and scale forms will correspond on any fret for all keys.

Guide Tone Voicings

Corresponding Scale Forms

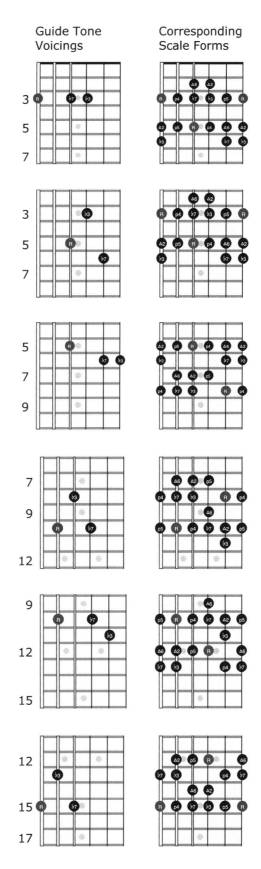

Dominant 7 Guide Tone Voicings and Corresponding Mixolydian Scale Forms

Fret numbers are applied to G dominant 7 but the chord and scale forms will correspond on any fret for all keys.

Guide Tone Voicings

Corresponding Scale Forms

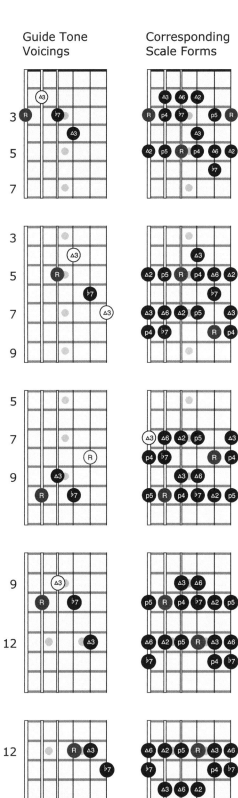

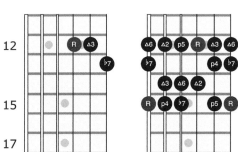

Pentatonic Scales

Pentatonic scales are some of the most common and useful scales for all styles of music. They are especially popular for guitarists as they are the foundation of blues and rock improvisation. The following pages will map the positions of the Major, Minor, and Dominant pentatonic scales. The page titled Pentatonic Applications also shows a Lydian Dominant Pentatonic and a Melodic Minor Pentatonic. Students can learn the forms of those two pentatonic by altering the Major, Minor, or Dominant pentatonic forms. It is important to understand the notes and intervals of these pentatonic scales in all twelve keys before implementing them.

Pentatonic Applications

Mahoney

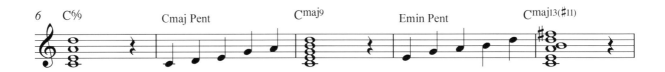

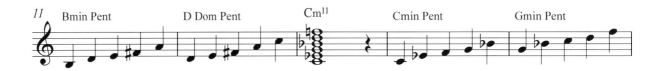

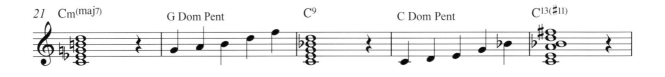

Major and Minor Pentatonic Forms

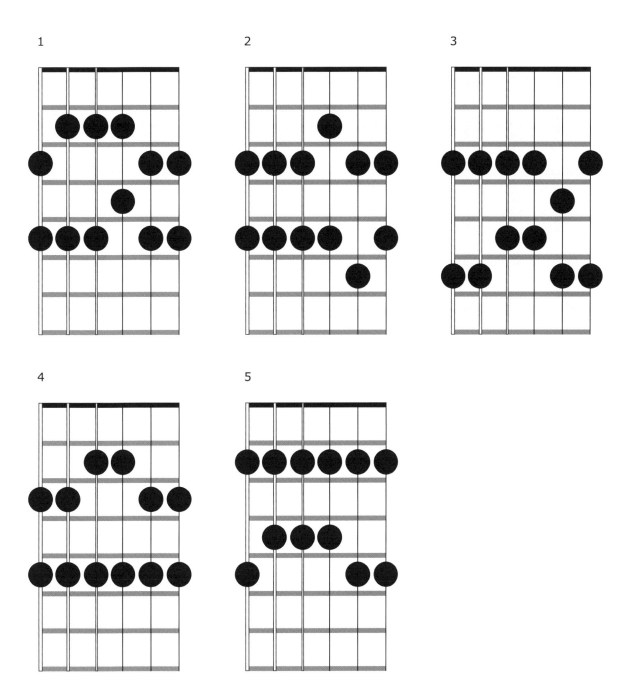

-The next pages will show how these scale forms apply to E minor and G major.
The forms can be moved up and down the neck to play the major and minor
pentatonic scales in all twelve keys.

Pentatonic Forms Side by Side

By visualizing these forms side by side, it becomes clear how the five forms interlock to connect the pentatonic scale through-out the entire neck. The forms repeat after the twelth fret.

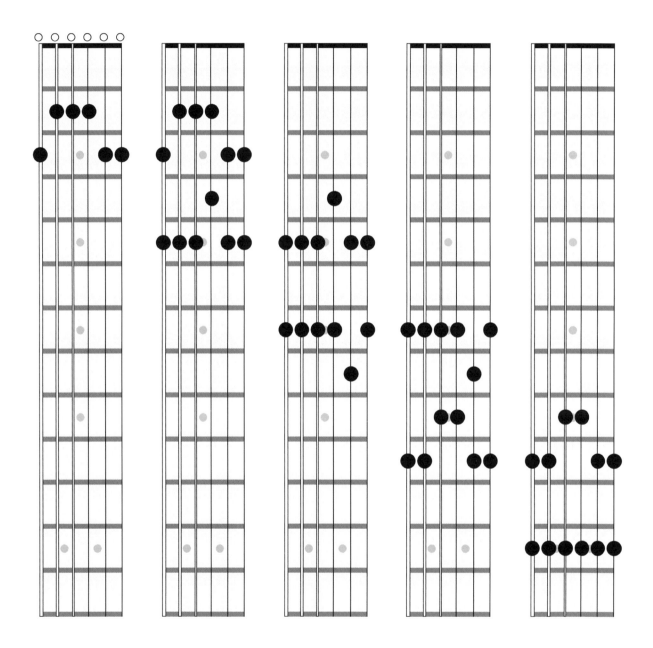

Five forms including scale degrees for G major pent:

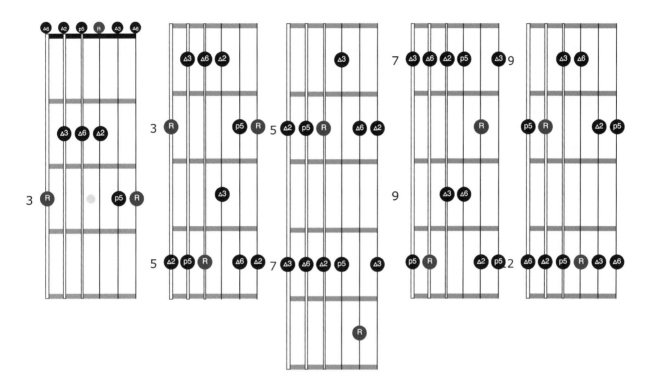

Five forms including note names for G major pent:

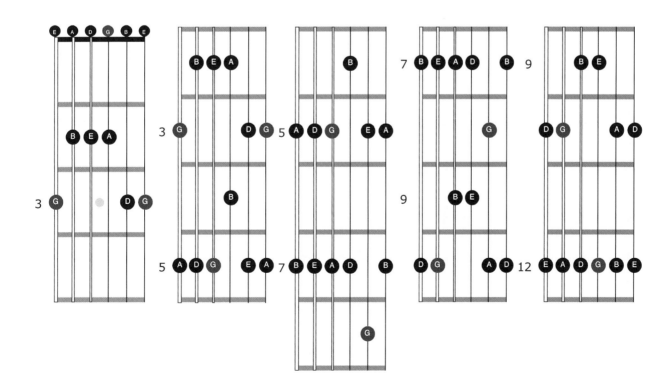

(E) Minor Pentatonic Forms

Five forms including scale degrees for E minor pent:

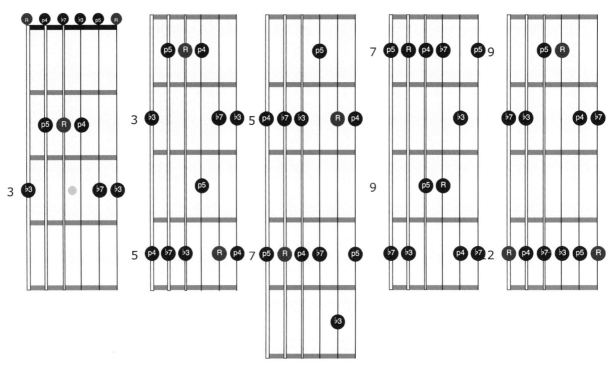

Five forms including note names for E minor pent:

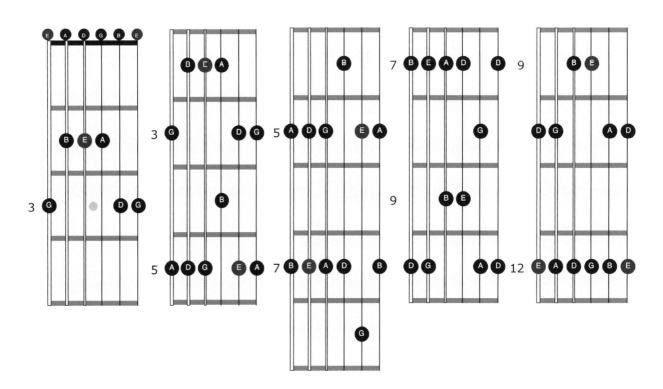

Dominant Pentatonic Forms

The Dominant Pentatonic is important for improvisation because of its use on
Dominant 7th and Altered Dominant (on the tritone) chords.

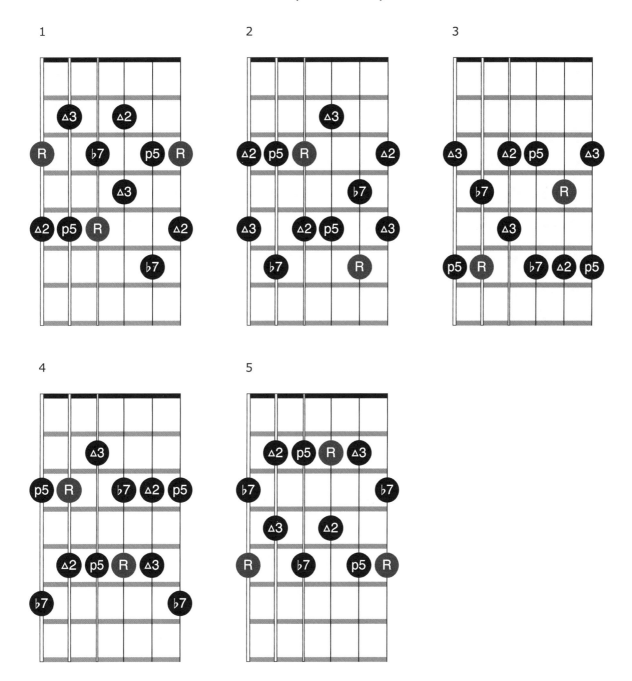

Dominant Pentatonic Forms Side by Side

By visualizing these forms side by side, it becomes clear how the five forms interlock to connect the dominant pentatonic scale throughout the entire neck. The forms repeat after the twelfth fret. The dominant pentatonic is presented here in the key of G but can be moved to any fret for different keys.

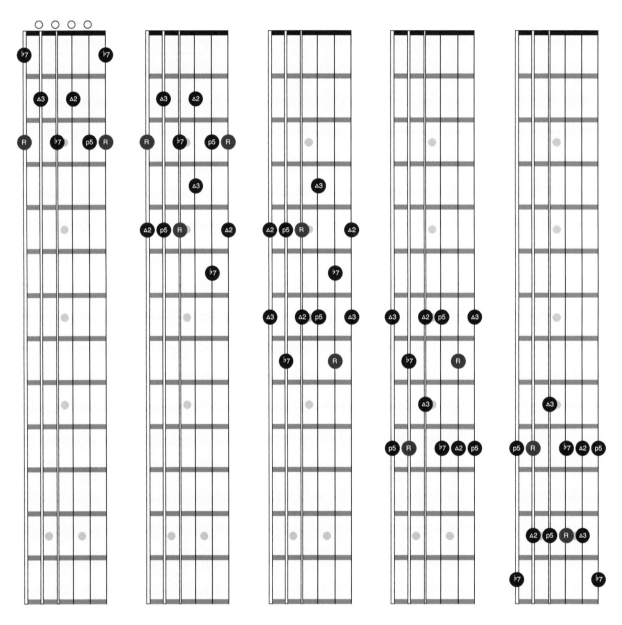

Dominant 7 Altered Voicings and Corresponding Dominant Pentatonic (Starting on the Tritone) Scale Forms.

Fret numbers are applied to G7alt but the chord and scale forms will correspond on any fret for all keys.

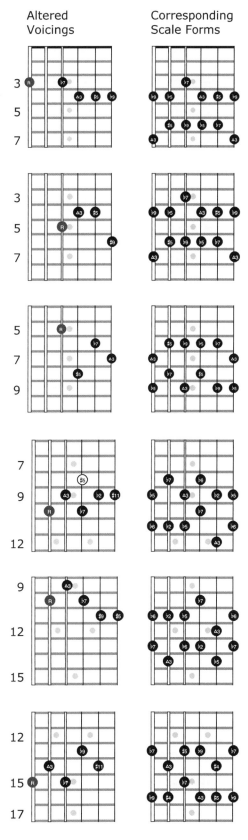

Melodic Minor Modes

The melodic minor modes are some of the most important tools for advanced improvisation. Its five most important modes correspond with five specific chords which include: minor/major7, dominant 7ths with #11, half diminished with natural 9, major 7th with #5, and altered dominant chords. Like the major scale forms, the melodic minor is divided into five forms on the fretboard.

Melodic Minor Scale Forms

These forms should be memorized in order to know the melodic minor scale and its modes. After understanding how the forms connect, the forms can be used to play the melodic minor and its modes in all 12 keys.

G Melodic Minor Forms Side by Side

Scale degree indications correspond with G melodic minor, or G -/maj7.

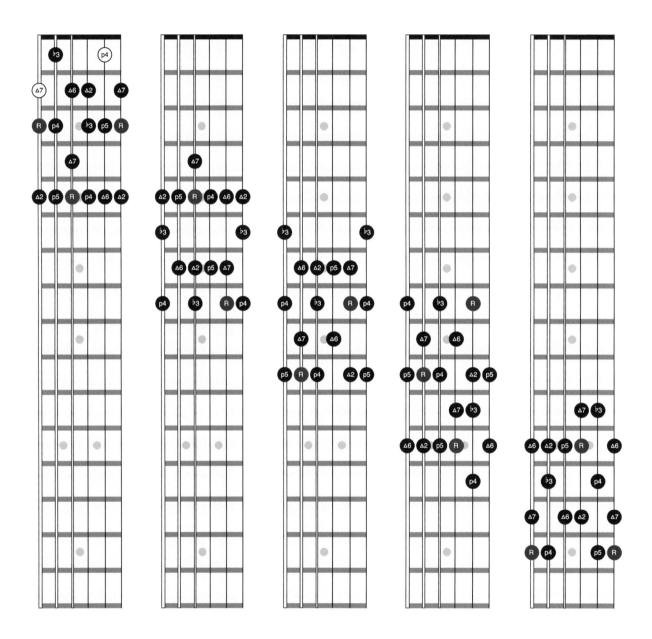

C Lydian Dominant Scale Forms Side by Side

Scale degree indications correspond with C lydian dominant scale, or C7#11.

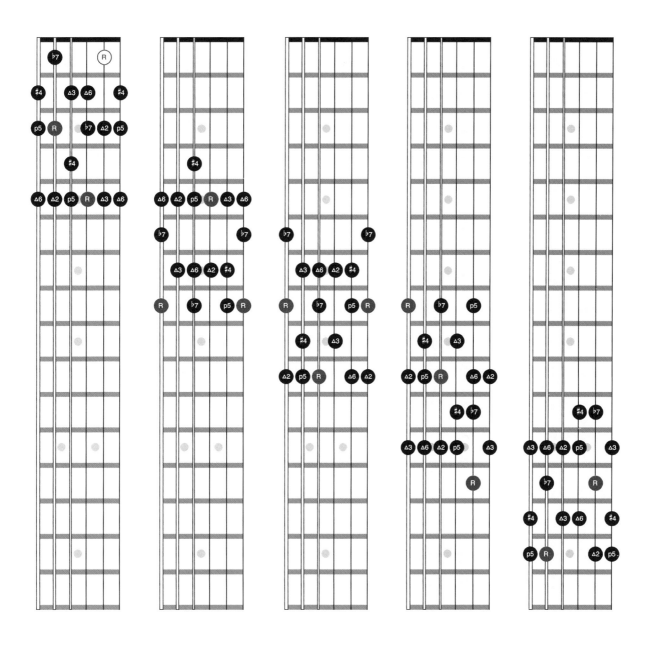

Bb lydian augmented Scale Forms Side by Side

Scale degree indications correspond with Bb lydian augmented scale,
or Bbmaj7(#5).

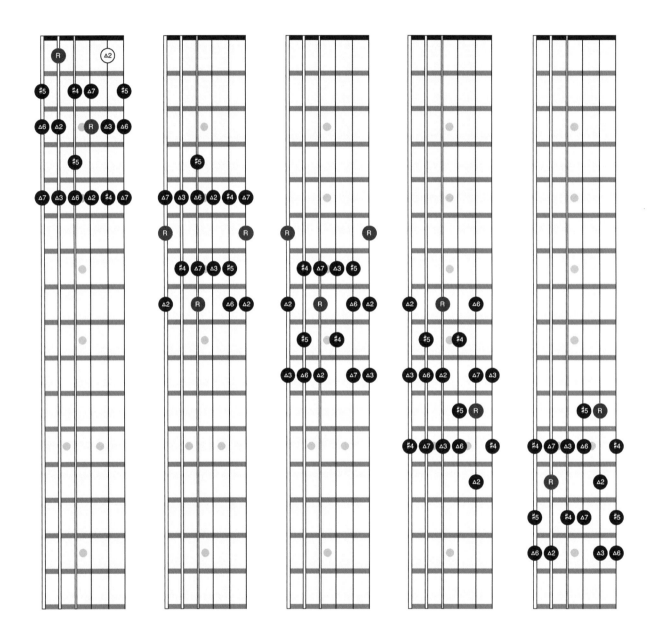

E locrian #2 Scale Forms Side by Side

Scale degree indications correspond with E locrian #2 scale, or E-7b5.

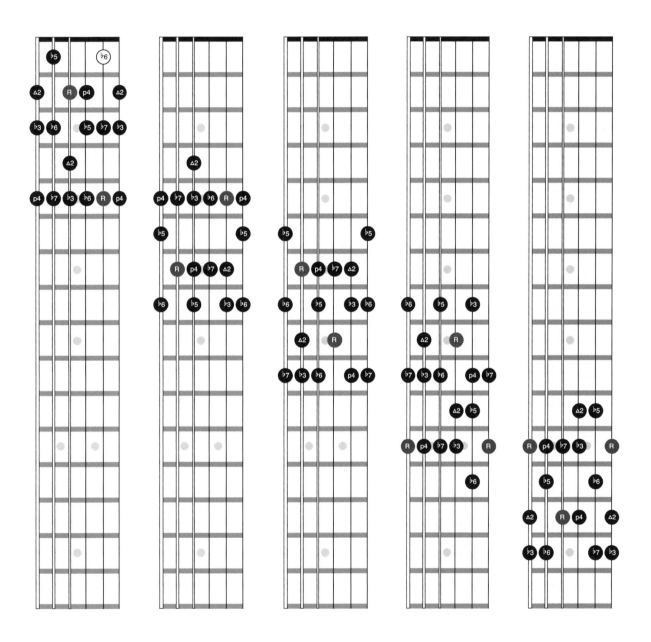

Gb Altered Scale Forms Side by Side

Scale degree indications correspond with Gb altered scale, or G7alt.

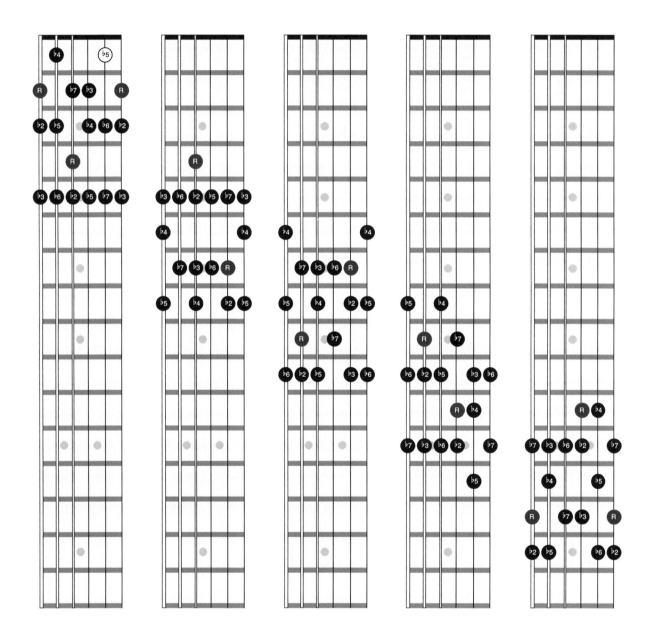

Dominant 7 Altered Voicings and Corresponding Altered Scale Forms

Fret numbers are applied to G7alt but the chord and scale forms will correspond on any fret for all keys.

Altered Voicings   Corresponding Scale Forms

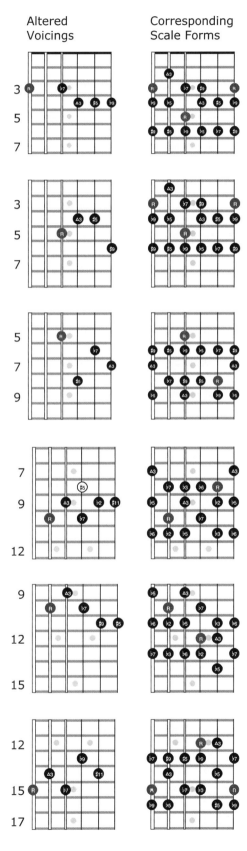

Harmonic Minor and Symmetrical Scales

Harmonic Minor – The harmonic minor is a useful and unique scale used in improvisation. It is especially good for using over dominant 7th chords with flat 9s and flat 13s. For dominant 7th with b9 and b13, play a harmonic minor scale a 5th down from the root of the chord. The use of the harmonic minor can be found in the improvisations of the bebop era of jazz music.

Symmetrical Scales – The symmetrical scales presented in this book are the diminished and whole tone scales. These are the most commonly used symmetrical scales. These scales are used for improvisation on diminished and dominant chords. The diminished and whole tone scales are especially fun to play on the guitar because of the symmetrical fretboard formations.

G Harmonic Minor Forms Side by Side

The presence of a minor 3rd from the b6 to the maj7 creates some challenging jumps and unusual fingerings within the harmonic minor forms.

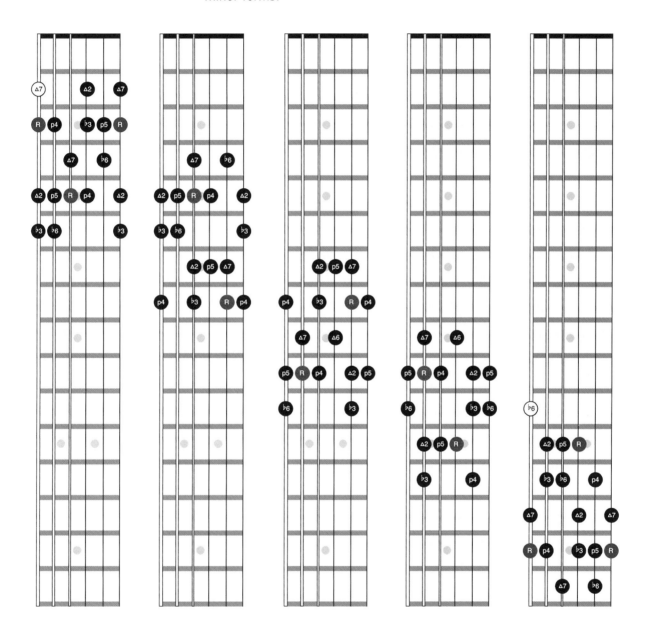

Whole Tone Scale Forms

The whole tone scale is used for augemented triads, augmented dominant 7th chords, and dominant 7th #11 chords.

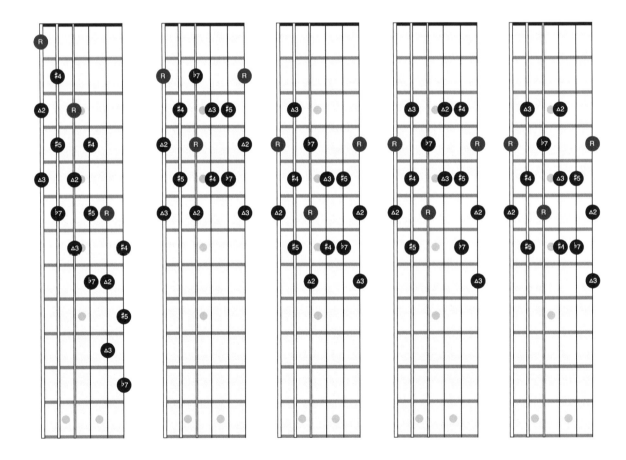

Symetrical Diminished Scale Forms

This scale can begin with either a whole step or a half step. The whole and half steps then alternate to complete the scale.

Whole-Half (1,2,b3,4,b5,b6,6,7):For Diminished 7th Chords

Half-Whole (1,b2,b3,3,b5,5,6,b7):For Dominant 7th (b5,b9,#9) Chords

(please note that there are many form possibilities for this scale. The forms presented are four notable fingerings)

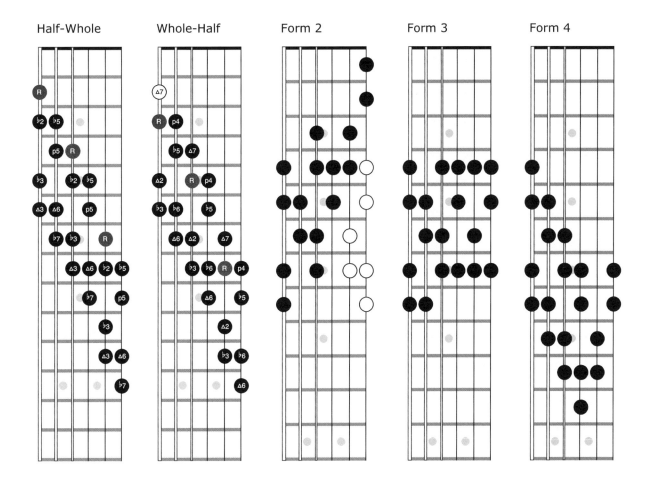

| Half-Whole | Whole-Half | Form 2 | Form 3 | Form 4 |

Major ii V I

Scale forms in relation to the ii-7(Dorian), V7alt(Altered), Imaj7#11(Lydian)
chord progression.

In this key (G), we have:
A dorian
   (A,B,C,D,E,F#,G)
D Altered
   (D, D#, F, F#, G#, Bb, C
G Lydian
   (G, A, B, C#, D, E, F#)

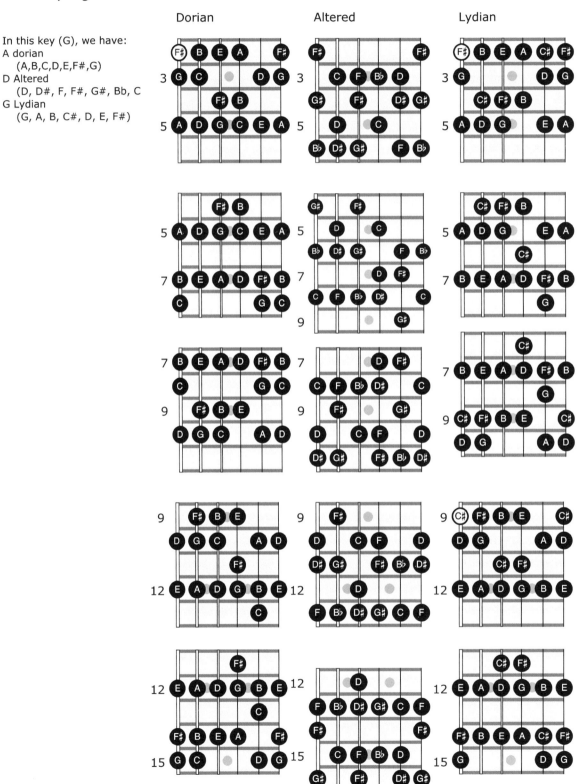

Minor ii V i

Scale forms in relation to the ii-7b5(Locrian#2), V7alt(Altered), i-7(Dorian) chord progression.

In this key (G), we have:
A Locrian#2
  (A,B,C,D,Eb,F,G)
D Altered
  (D, D#, F, F#, G#, Bb, C
G Dorian
  (G, A, Bb, C, D, E, F)

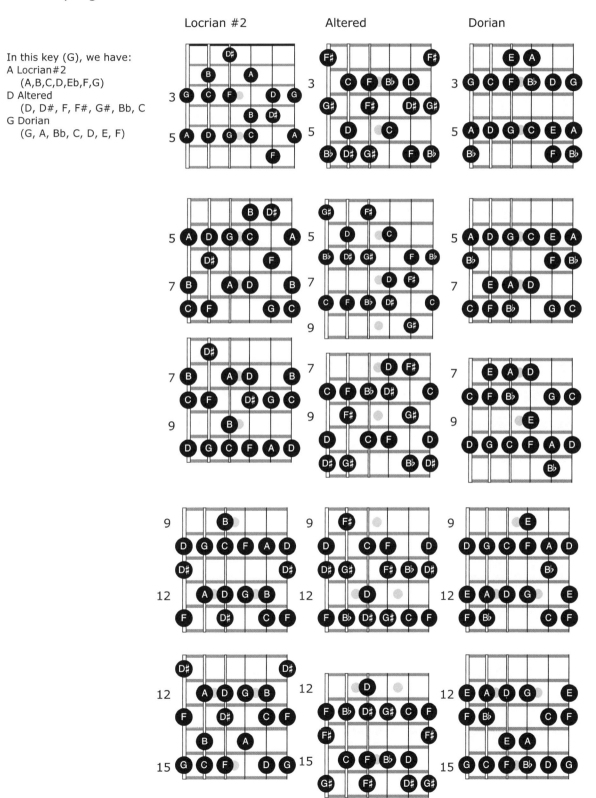

Chord Table

Triads

Chord	Structure	Notes	Pattern of Thirds
Major	1, 3, 5	G, B, D	M3+m3
Minor	1, b3, 5	G, Bb, D	m3+M3
Diminished	1, b3, b5	G, Bb, Db	m3+m3
Augmented	1, 3, #5	G, B, D#	M3+M3

Seventh Chords

Chord	Structure	Note	Pattern of Thirds
Major7	1, 3, 5, 7	G, B, D, F#	M3+m3+M3
Minor7	1, b3, 5, b7	G, Bb, D, F	m3+M3+m3
Dominant7	1, 3, 5, b7	G, B, D, F	M3+m3+m3

Seventh chords are the foundation of jazz harmony. They can be divided into three families; Major, Minor, and Dominant. The 3rd and 7th of seventh chords are the **guide tones**. The root(1) and 5th do not change between major minor and dominant, and therefore the guide tones are what differentiates and defines major minor and dominant seventh chords.

*Using numbers to represent the chord tones and extensions is common and is an effective way to understand chord and scale structures.

Chord Extensions

Major, Minor, and Dominant 7th chords can be extended with 9ths, 11ths, and 13ths. Those extensions can then be altered by raising or lowering with sharps and flats. For example, #9, b9, #11, b13, etc. These variations create an abundance of harmonic possibilities and applications. The chords and their extensions also determine what scales fit each chord. Common chord extension applications are illustrated in the following charts:

Major:

Chord	Structure	Possible Extensions	Notes
Major7	1, 3, 5, 7	9, 13, #11	G, B, D, F# (A, E, C#)
Major6	1, 3, 5, 6	9, #11	G, B, D, E (A, C#)
Major7 #5	1, 3, #5, 7	9, 13, #11	G, B, D#, F# (A, E, C#)

Minor:

Chord	Structure	Possible Extensions	Notes
Minor7	1, b3, 5, b7	9, 11, 13	G, Bb, D, F (A, E, C)
Minor6	1, b3, 5, 6	9, 11	G, Bb, D, E (A, C)
Minor7b5(half-dim)	1, b3, b5, b7	9, b9, #5(b13), 11	G, Bb, Db, F (A, Ab Eb, C)
Minor/maj7	1, b3, 5, 7	9, 11, 13	G, Bb, D, F# (A, E, C)

Dominant:

Chord	Structure	Possible Extensions	Notes
Dominant7	1, 3, 5, b7	9, 13	G, B, D, F, A, E
Dominant7suspended	1, 4, 5, b7	9, 13	G, C, D, F, A, E
Dominant7#11	1, 3, 5, b7	9, #11, 13	G, B, D, F, A, C#, E
Dominant13b9	1, 3, 5, b7	b9, #9, #11, 13	G, B, D, F, (Ab, A#, C#, E
Aug Dominant9	1, 3, #5, b7	9, #11	G, B, D#, F, A, C#
Altered Dominant7	1, 3, b7	#9, b9, #5(b13), #11	G, B, D#, F, (Ab, A#, C#)
Diminished7	1, b3, b5, bb7	7, 9, 11	G, Bb, Db, Fb, F#, A, C

CPSIA information can be obtained at www.ICGtesting.com
Printed in the USA
LVIW01n1515281117
557884LV00011B/195